Teach Your Child to Read
300 Short Easy Sentences

English - Filipino

Name

I Can...

- [ ] read the 1st sentence.
- [ ] read the 2nd sentence.
- [ ] make a sentence from a picture.
- [ ] color a picture.
- [ ] Draw a picture.

The frog is going to a party.

Ang palaka ay pupunta sa isang partido.

The happy frog is wearing a green hat.

Ang masayang palaka ay may suot na berdeng sumbrero.

Name

I Can...

- [ ] read the 1st sentence.
- [ ] read the 2nd sentence.
- [ ] make a sentence from a picture.
- [ ] color a picture.
- [ ] Draw a picture.

Owl likes to read big books.

Mahilig magbasa ng malaking libro si Owl.

A smart owl is reading an alphabet book.

Ang isang matalinong kuwago ay nagbabasa ng isang aklat ng alpabeto.

Name

I Can...

- [ ] read the 1st sentence.
- [ ] read the 2nd sentence.
- [ ] make a sentence from a picture.
- [ ] color a picture.
- [ ] Draw a picture.

Come on! The ice cream truck is here!

Halika na! Narito ang ice cream truck!

He is driving a big icecream truck.

Nagmamaneho siya ng isang malaking trak na icecream.

Name

I Can...

- [ ] read the 1st sentence.
- [ ] read the 2nd sentence.
- [ ] make a sentence from a picture.
- [ ] color a picture.
- [ ] Draw a picture.

Dragons are very friendly and have scales on their backs.

Ang mga dragon ay napaka-friendly at may mga kaliskis sa kanilang mga likod.

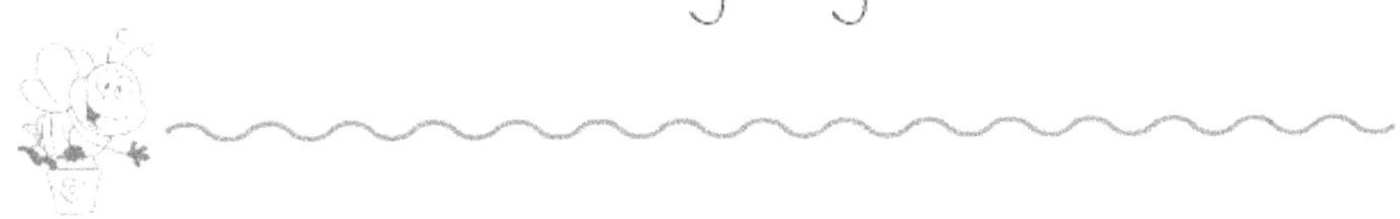

The dragon is waving his hand.

Ang dragon ay kumakaway sa kanyang kamay.

Name

I Can...

- [ ] read the 1st sentence.
- [ ] read the 2nd sentence.
- [ ] make a sentence from a picture.
- [ ] color a picture.
- [ ] Draw a picture.

This ram lives in the farmhouse.

Ang ram na ito ay nakatira sa farmhouse.

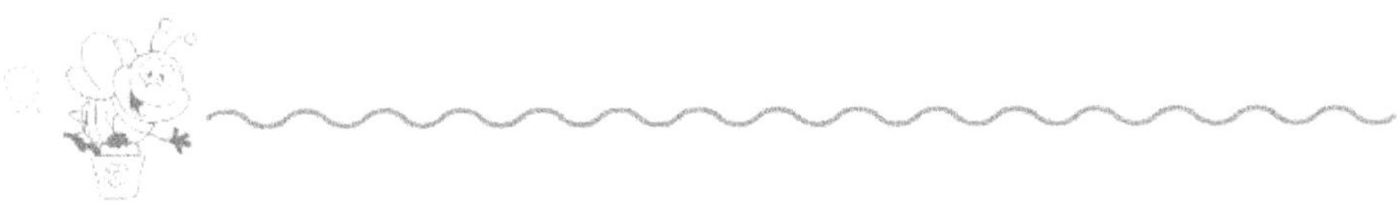

Ram has a large horn and fluffy wool.

Si Ram ay may malaking sungay at malambot na lana.

Name

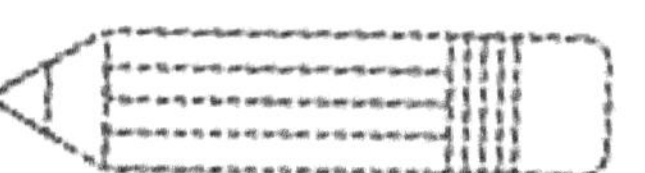

I Can...

- [ ] read the 1st sentence.
- [ ] read the 2nd sentence.
- [ ] make a sentence from a picture.
- [ ] color a picture.
- [ ] Draw a picture.

The bunny likes to eat carrots.

Mahilig kumain ng karot ang kuneho.

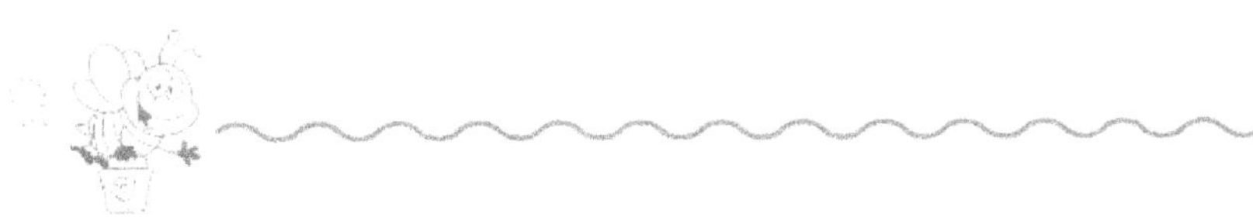

Rabbit thinks that the juicy orange carrot looks yummy.

Iniisip ni Kuneho na ang makatas na orange na karot ay mukhang masarap.

Name

I Can...

- ☐ read the 1st sentence.
- ☐ read the 2nd sentence.
- ☐ make a sentence from a picture.
- ☐ color a picture.
- ☐ Draw a picture.

The clown likes to give out balloons to little kids.

Gusto ng payaso na magbigay ng mga lobo sa maliliit na bata.

Funny, Mr. Clown is giving away colorful balloons.

Nakakatawa, binibigyan ni G. Clown ang mga makukulay na lobo.

Name

I Can...

- ☐ read the 1st sentence.
- ☐ read the 2nd sentence.
- ☐ make a sentence from a picture.
- ☐ color a picture.
- ☐ Draw a picture.

The clown is juggling balls for his performance.

Ang clown ay juggling ball para sa kanyang pagganap.

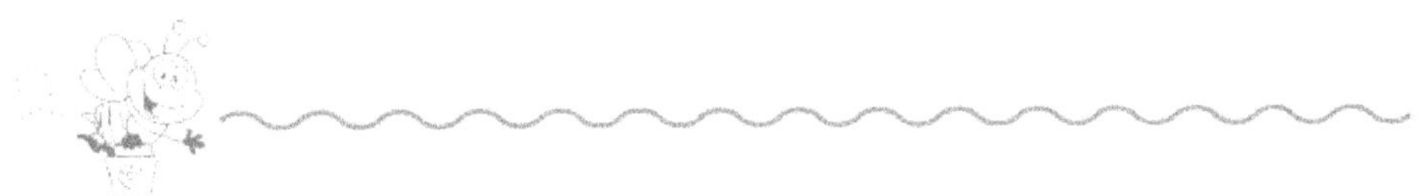

Talented, Mr. Clown is juggling five red balls.

Nabati, si G. Clown ay nag-juggling ng limang pulang bola.

Name _______________ 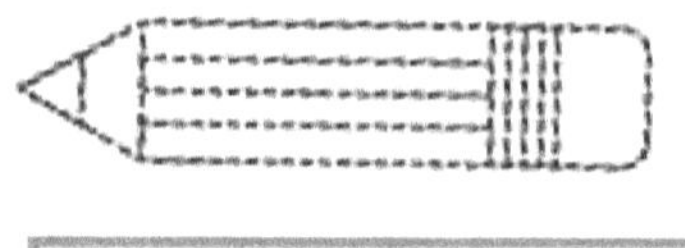

I Can...

- [ ] read the 1st sentence.
- [ ] read the 2nd sentence.
- [ ] make a sentence from a picture.
- [ ] color a picture.
- [ ] Draw a picture.

The Easter Bunny is going to give out chocolate eggs.

Ang Easter Bunny ay magbibigay ng mga itlog ng tsokolate.

The rabbit goes out to buy more orange carrots.

Lumabas ang kuneho upang bumili ng higit pang mga orange na karot.

Name

I Can...

- [ ] read the 1st sentence.
- [ ] read the 2nd sentence.
- [ ] make a sentence from a picture.
- [ ] color a picture.
- [ ] Draw a picture.

The pencil is drawing a zig-zag line.

Ang lapis ay pagguhit ng isang linya ng zig-zag.

The Pencil is saying hello to you.

Kumusta ang lapis sa iyo ng Pencil.

Name ___________________

I Can...

- [ ] read the 1st sentence.
- [ ] read the 2nd sentence.
- [ ] make a sentence from a picture.
- [ ] color a picture.
- [ ] Draw a picture.

The pencil put on a big smile and went to work.

Ang lapis ay nakasuot ng isang malaking ngiti at nagtatrabaho.

The Pencil is leaving to go on a long relaxing vacation.

Aalis ang Pencil upang pumunta sa isang mahabang nakakarelaks na bakasyon.

Name ____________________ 

I Can...

- [ ] read the 1st sentence.
- [ ] read the 2nd sentence.
- [ ] make a sentence from a picture.
- [ ] color a picture.
- [ ] Draw a picture.

This snowman is my friend, and he is a helper of Santa.

Ang taong yari sa niyebe na ito ay aking kaibigan, at siya ay isang katulong sa Santa.

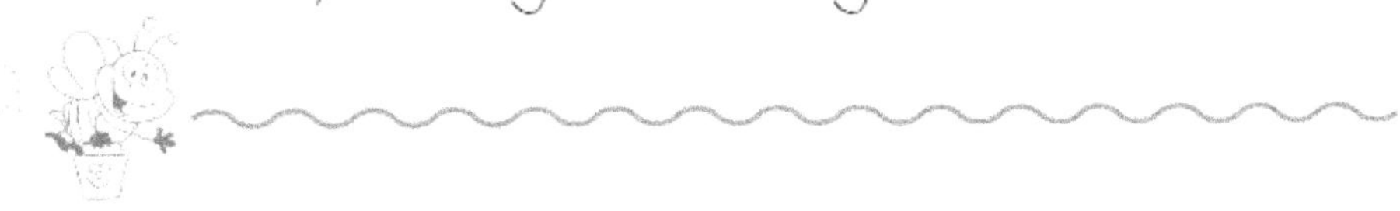

Mr. Snowman is celebrating Christmas by the decorated tree.

Ipinagdiriwang ni G. Snowman ang Pasko ng pinalamutian na puno.

Name

I Can...

- [ ] read the 1st sentence.
- [ ] read the 2nd sentence.
- [ ] make a sentence from a picture.
- [ ] color a picture.
- [ ] Draw a picture.

The octopus is working as a chef and serving food.

Ang pugita ay gumagana bilang isang chef at paghahatid ng pagkain.

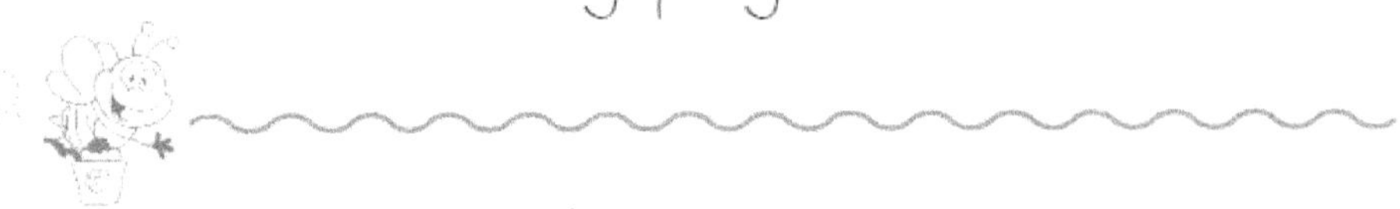

Chef Octopus is serving a delicious turkey dinner.

Ang Chef Octopus ay naghahain ng masarap na hapunan ng pabo.

Name

I Can...

- [ ] read the 1st sentence.
- [ ] read the 2nd sentence.
- [ ] make a sentence from a picture.
- [ ] color a picture.
- [ ] Draw a picture.

Santa is happy.

Masaya si Santa.

Santa Claus is giving extraordinary presents to excited kids.

Nagbibigay ang Santa Claus ng pambihirang regalo sa mga excited na bata.

Name

I Can...

- ☐ read the 1st sentence.
- ☐ read the 2nd sentence.
- ☐ make a sentence from a picture.
- ☐ color a picture.
- ☐ Draw a picture.

The bear likes to eat sweets.

Mahilig kumain ng mga matatamis ang oso.

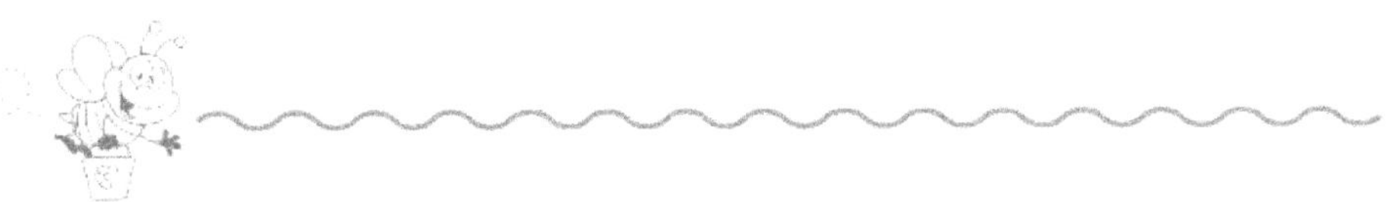

Teddy is licking a red and white candy cane.

Si Teddy ay nagdila ng isang pula at puting kendi na tubo.

Name

I Can...

- [ ] read the 1st sentence.
- [ ] read the 2nd sentence.
- [ ] make a sentence from a picture.
- [ ] color a picture.
- [ ] Draw a picture.

The book has a wand.

May libog ang libro.

The cereal box got a magician set for Christmas.

Ang butil ng cereal ay nakakuha ng isang set ng mago para sa Pasko.

Name

I Can...

- [ ] read the 1st sentence.
- [ ] read the 2nd sentence.
- [ ] make a sentence from a picture.
- [ ] color a picture.
- [ ] Draw a picture.

The bear has a present.

Ang oso ay may isang kasalukuyan.

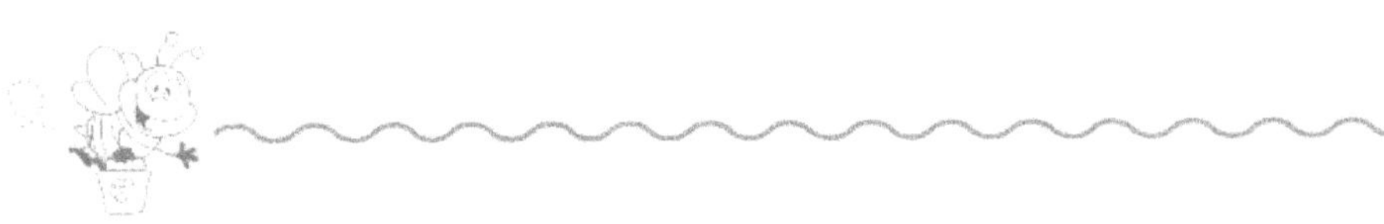

Happy Teddy is opening his box of presents from Santa.

Maligayang Teddy ang pagbubukas ng kanyang kahon ng mga regalo mula sa Santa.

I Can...

- [ ] read the 1st sentence.
- [ ] read the 2nd sentence.
- [ ] make a sentence from a picture.
- [ ] color a picture.
- [ ] Draw a picture.

Santa is going to give out presents.

Si Santa ay magbibigay ng mga regalo.

Santa is lugging a large brown bag of gifts to his sley.

Si Santa ay naghahawak ng isang malaking brown bag ng mga regalo sa kanyang sley.

Name 

I Can...

- [ ] read the 1st sentence.
- [ ] read the 2nd sentence.
- [ ] make a sentence from a picture.
- [ ] color a picture.
- [ ] Draw a picture.

I made a snowman.

Gumawa ako ng snowman.

Mr. Snowman is holding a broom and saying goodbye.

Si G. Snowman ay may hawak na walis at nagpaalam.

Name

I Can...

- [ ] read the 1st sentence.
- [ ] read the 2nd sentence.
- [ ] make a sentence from a picture.
- [ ] color a picture.
- [ ] Draw a picture.

The parrot is colorful.

Makulay ang loro.

The green parrot came from the forest to the zoo.

Ang berdeng loro ay nagmula sa kagubatan hanggang sa zoo.

Name 

I Can...

- [ ] read the 1st sentence.
- [ ] read the 2nd sentence.
- [ ] make a sentence from a picture.
- [ ] color a picture.
- [ ] Draw a picture.

There are a lot of animals.

Maraming mga hayop.

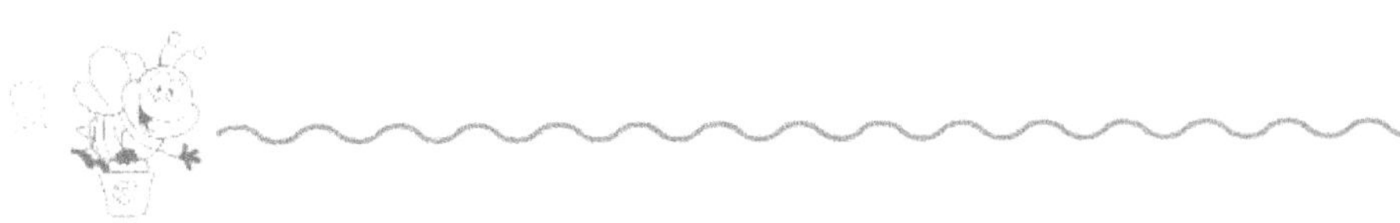

The animals are happy being together again.

Ang mga hayop ay masaya na muling magkasama.

Name

I Can...

- [ ] read the 1st sentence.
- [ ] read the 2nd sentence.
- [ ] make a sentence from a picture.
- [ ] color a picture.
- [ ] Draw a picture.

The man is wearing a belt.

Ang lalaki ay may suot na sinturon.

The carpenter is fixing something.

Ang karpintero ay nag-aayos ng isang bagay.

Name

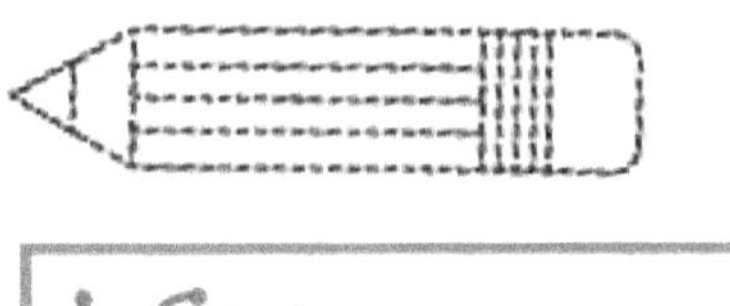

I Can...

- [ ] read the 1st sentence.
- [ ] read the 2nd sentence.
- [ ] make a sentence from a picture.
- [ ] color a picture.
- [ ] Draw a picture.

The rabbit is very young.

Napakabata ng kuneho.

The magician plays a trick.

Ang salamangkero ay gumaganap ng isang trick.

Name

I Can...

- [ ] read the 1st sentence.
- [ ] read the 2nd sentence.
- [ ] make a sentence from a picture.
- [ ] color a picture.
- [ ] Draw a picture.

He has a potion.

May potion siya.

The scientist is making a potion.

Ang siyentipiko ay gumagawa ng isang potion.

Name

I Can...

- [ ] read the 1st sentence.
- [ ] read the 2nd sentence.
- [ ] make a sentence from a picture.
- [ ] color a picture.
- [ ] Draw a picture.

He is wearing sunglasses.

Nakasuot siya ng salaming pang-araw.

The policeman is mad.

Galit ang pulis.

Name

26

I Can...

- [ ] read the 1st sentence.
- [ ] read the 2nd sentence.
- [ ] make a sentence from a picture.
- [ ] color a picture.
- [ ] Draw a picture.

He has a bucket of paint.

May balde siyang pintura.

He likes to paint.

Mahilig siyang magpinta.

Name

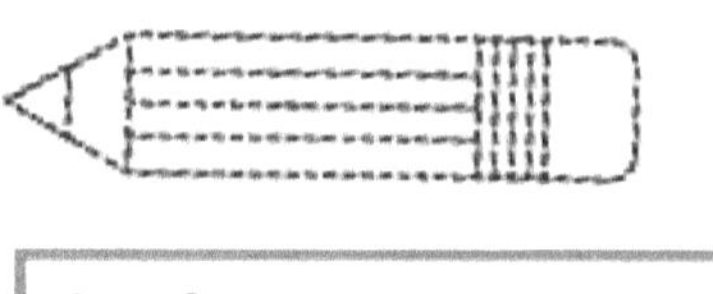

I Can...

- [ ] read the 1st sentence.
- [ ] read the 2nd sentence.
- [ ] make a sentence from a picture.
- [ ] color a picture.
- [ ] Draw a picture.

The man has a hat.

May sumbrero ang lalaki.

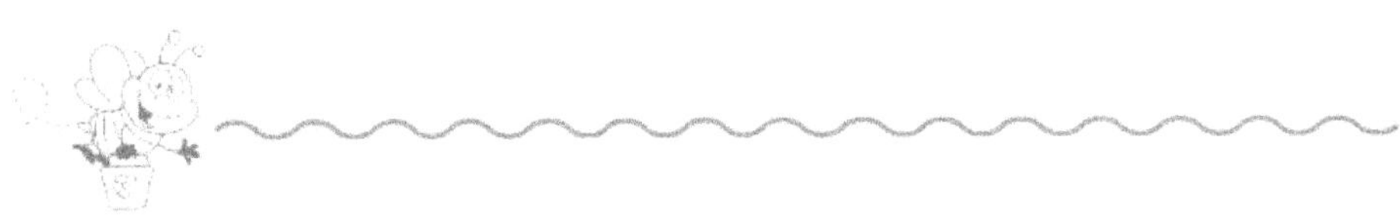

The postman is giving out the mail in the early morning.

Ang postman ay nagbibigay ng mail sa umaga.

Name

I Can...

- [ ] read the 1st sentence.
- [ ] read the 2nd sentence.
- [ ] make a sentence from a picture.
- [ ] color a picture.
- [ ] Draw a picture.

He has a walkie talkie.

May walkie talkie siya.

He is going to work with his suitcase.

Pupunta siya sa kanyang maleta.

Name

I Can...

- [ ] read the 1st sentence.
- [ ] read the 2nd sentence.
- [ ] make a sentence from a picture.
- [ ] color a picture.
- [ ] Draw a picture.

He is sleepy.

Inaantok siya.

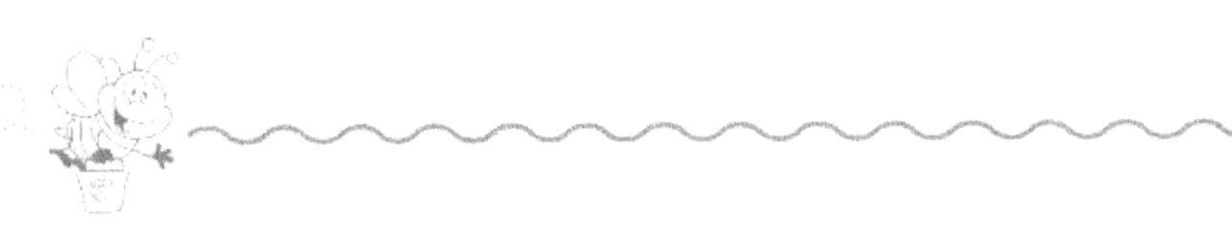

The delivery man sent us a package.

Nagpadala sa amin ang isang tao ng paghahatid ng isang pakete.

Name

I Can...

- [ ] read the 1st sentence.
- [ ] read the 2nd sentence.
- [ ] make a sentence from a picture.
- [ ] color a picture.
- [ ] Draw a picture.

He is wearing a bowtie.

Nakasuot siya ng bowtie.

The waiter is serving juice.

Ang waiter ay naghahain ng juice.

Name

I Can...

- [ ] read the 1st sentence.
- [ ] read the 2nd sentence.
- [ ] make a sentence from a picture.
- [ ] color a picture.
- [ ] Draw a picture.

He has a suitcase.

May maleta siya.

The engineer is holding a wrench.

Ang engineer ay may hawak na wrench.

I Can...

- [ ] read the 1st sentence.
- [ ] read the 2nd sentence.
- [ ] make a sentence from a picture.
- [ ] color a picture.
- [ ] Draw a picture.

The chef has a napkin.

Ang chef ay may napkin.

The chef serves delicious-looking food.

Naghahain ang chef ng masarap na pagkain.

Name

I Can...

- [ ] read the 1st sentence.
- [ ] read the 2nd sentence.
- [ ] make a sentence from a picture.
- [ ] color a picture.
- [ ] Draw a picture.

The rooster has a big beak.

Ang tandang ay may isang malaking tuka.

The chicken is saying hello to us.

Kumusta ang manok sa amin.

Name

I Can...

- ☐ read the 1st sentence.
- ☐ read the 2nd sentence.
- ☐ make a sentence from a picture.
- ☐ color a picture.
- ☐ Draw a picture.

The bird is small.

Maliit ang ibon.

The chick is on the telephone talking with his friend.

Ang sisiw ay nasa telepono na nakikipag-usap sa kanyang kaibigan.

Name

I Can...

- [ ] read the 1st sentence.
- [ ] read the 2nd sentence.
- [ ] make a sentence from a picture.
- [ ] color a picture.
- [ ] Draw a picture.

That is my ring.

Iyon ang aking singsing.

That is a beautiful ring.

Iyon ay isang magandang singsing.

Name

I Can...

- [ ] read the 1st sentence.
- [ ] read the 2nd sentence.
- [ ] make a sentence from a picture.
- [ ] color a picture.
- [ ] Draw a picture.

The duck has three eggs.

Ang pato ay may tatlong itlog.

The duck has a big nose.

May malaking ilong ang pato.

Name

I Can...

- [ ] read the 1st sentence.
- [ ] read the 2nd sentence.
- [ ] make a sentence from a picture.
- [ ] color a picture.
- [ ] Draw a picture.

The swan is beautiful.

Ang swan ay maganda.

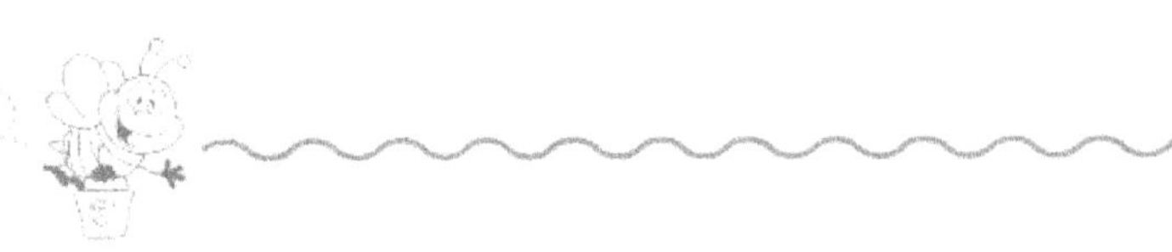

The graceful swan is striding through the water.

Ang kaaya-aya na swan ay tumatakbo sa tubig.

Name

I Can...

- ☐ read the 1st sentence.
- ☐ read the 2nd sentence.
- ☐ make a sentence from a picture.
- ☐ color a picture.
- ☐ Draw a picture.

The girl is wearing a dress.

Nakasuot ng damit ang babae.

The maid is cleaning our room.

Naglilinis ang dalaga sa aming silid.

Name

I Can...

- [ ] read the 1st sentence.
- [ ] read the 2nd sentence.
- [ ] make a sentence from a picture.
- [ ] color a picture.
- [ ] Draw a picture.

The boy is running.

Tumatakbo ang batang lalaki.

The little boy was running.

Tumatakbo ang maliit na batang lalaki.

Name

I Can...

- [ ] read the 1st sentence.
- [ ] read the 2nd sentence.
- [ ] make a sentence from a picture.
- [ ] color a picture.
- [ ] Draw a picture.

He is a musician.

Siya ay isang musikero.

He is playing a lively tune on his flute.

Siya ay naglalaro ng isang buhay na buhay na himig sa kanyang plauta.

Name _______________

I Can...

- [ ] read the 1st sentence.
- [ ] read the 2nd sentence.
- [ ] make a sentence from a picture.
- [ ] color a picture.
- [ ] Draw a picture.

He looks joyful.

Mukha siyang natutuwa.

That boy works in a band and plays the drum.

Ang batang iyon ay nagtatrabaho sa isang banda at gumaganap ng tambol.

Name

I Can...

- [ ] read the 1st sentence.
- [ ] read the 2nd sentence.
- [ ] make a sentence from a picture.
- [ ] color a picture.
- [ ] Draw a picture.

The dinosaur is a rock star.

Ang dinosaur ay isang rock star.

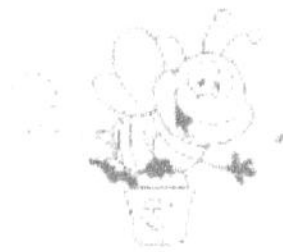

____

The dragon is playing the guitar.

Naglalaro ang gitara ng gitara.

Name

I Can...

- [ ] read the 1st sentence.
- [ ] read the 2nd sentence.
- [ ] make a sentence from a picture.
- [ ] color a picture.
- [ ] Draw a picture.

The nurse helps the doctor.

Tumutulong ang nars sa doktor.

The nurse looks scary, holding a syringe.

Nakakatakot ang nars, may hawak na syringe.

Name

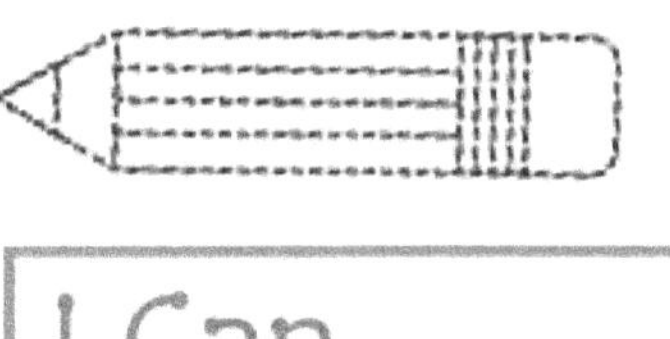

I Can...

- [ ] read the 1st sentence.
- [ ] read the 2nd sentence.
- [ ] make a sentence from a picture.
- [ ] color a picture.
- [ ] Draw a picture.

She is wearing a crown.

May suot siyang korona.

The queen bee has a beautiful wand.

May magandang wand ang reyna ng reyna.

Name

I Can...

- [ ] read the 1st sentence.
- [ ] read the 2nd sentence.
- [ ] make a sentence from a picture.
- [ ] color a picture.
- [ ] Draw a picture.

It is orange and black.

Ito ay orange at itim.

The tiger is wearing a bow on its neck.

Ang tigre ay may suot na busog sa leeg nito.

Name

I Can...

- [ ] read the 1st sentence.
- [ ] read the 2nd sentence.
- [ ] make a sentence from a picture.
- [ ] color a picture.
- [ ] Draw a picture.

The boy is carrying a lot of books.

Ang bata ay nagdadala ng maraming mga libro.

The boy is carrying so many books!

Ang batang lalaki ay nagdadala ng maraming mga libro!

Name

I Can...

- [ ] read the 1st sentence.
- [ ] read the 2nd sentence.
- [ ] make a sentence from a picture.
- [ ] color a picture.
- [ ] Draw a picture.

The pizza looks delicious.

Masarap ang pizza.

The waiter is serving steaming hot pizza.

Ang weyter ay naghahain ng steaming hot pizza.

Name _______________

I Can...

- ☐ read the 1st sentence.
- ☐ read the 2nd sentence.
- ☐ make a sentence from a picture.
- ☐ color a picture.
- ☐ Draw a picture.

That is my dad's computer.

Iyon ang computer ng aking tatay.

My dad works on the computer.

Nagtatrabaho ang aking tatay sa computer.

Name

I Can...

- [ ] read the 1st sentence.
- [ ] read the 2nd sentence.
- [ ] make a sentence from a picture.
- [ ] color a picture.
- [ ] Draw a picture.

The farmer has a beard.

Ang magsasaka ay may balbas.

The gardener is going to plant flowers

Ang hardinero ay magtatanim ng mga bulaklak

I Can...

- [ ] read the 1st sentence.
- [ ] read the 2nd sentence.
- [ ] make a sentence from a picture.
- [ ] color a picture.
- [ ] Draw a picture.

The strawberry is red.

Pula ang strawberry.

 ___________________________

I love to drink strawberry juice.

Mahilig akong uminom ng strawberry juice.

Name

I Can...

- [ ] read the 1st sentence.
- [ ] read the 2nd sentence.
- [ ] make a sentence from a picture.
- [ ] color a picture.
- [ ] Draw a picture.

The magician has a wand.

Ang salamangkero ay may isang wand.

The wizard likes to work with magic.

Gusto ng wizard na gumana sa magic.

Name

I Can...

- [ ] read the 1st sentence.
- [ ] read the 2nd sentence.
- [ ] make a sentence from a picture.
- [ ] color a picture.
- [ ] Draw a picture.

Reindeer has a scarf.

May scarf si Reindeer.

Santa gave reindeer a big present.

Bigyan ng regalo si Santa sa reindeer.

Name

I Can...

- [ ] read the 1st sentence.
- [ ] read the 2nd sentence.
- [ ] make a sentence from a picture.
- [ ] color a picture.
- [ ] Draw a picture.

I have a lot of pencils.

Marami akong lapis.

I have a lot of brushes and pencils.

Marami akong brushes at lapis.

Name

I Can...

- [ ] read the 1st sentence.
- [ ] read the 2nd sentence.
- [ ] make a sentence from a picture.
- [ ] color a picture.
- [ ] Draw a picture.

Santa is fat.

Mataba si Santa.

Santa is having fun.

Nakakatuwa si Santa.

I Can...

- [ ] read the 1st sentence.
- [ ] read the 2nd sentence.
- [ ] make a sentence from a picture.
- [ ] color a picture.
- [ ] Draw a picture.

I have one nose.

Mayroon akong isang ilong.

The one is saying its name.

Sinasabi ng isa ang pangalan nito.

Name

I Can...

- [ ] read the 1st sentence.
- [ ] read the 2nd sentence.
- [ ] make a sentence from a picture.
- [ ] color a picture.
- [ ] Draw a picture.

I have two ears.

Mayroon akong dalawang tainga.

The number "two" is holding up bunny ears.

Ang bilang na "dalawa" ay humahawak ng mga maliliit na tainga.

Name

I Can...

- [ ] read the 1st sentence.
- [ ] read the 2nd sentence.
- [ ] make a sentence from a picture.
- [ ] color a picture.
- [ ] Draw a picture.

I have three buttons on my dress.

Mayroon akong tatlong mga pindutan sa aking damit.

The number "three" is saying you got 3 out of 3.

Ang bilang na "tatlo" ay nagsasabi na mayroon kang 3 sa 3.

Name

I Can...

- [ ] read the 1st sentence.
- [ ] read the 2nd sentence.
- [ ] make a sentence from a picture.
- [ ] color a picture.
- [ ] Draw a picture.

I have 0 tails.

Mayroon akong 0 buntot.

The number "zero" is saying, Ok.

Ang bilang ng "zero" ay sinasabi, Ok.

Name _______________________

I Can...

- [ ] read the 1st sentence.
- [ ] read the 2nd sentence.
- [ ] make a sentence from a picture.
- [ ] color a picture.
- [ ] Draw a picture.

I have five fingers on 1 of my hands.

Mayroon akong limang daliri sa 1 ng aking mga kamay.

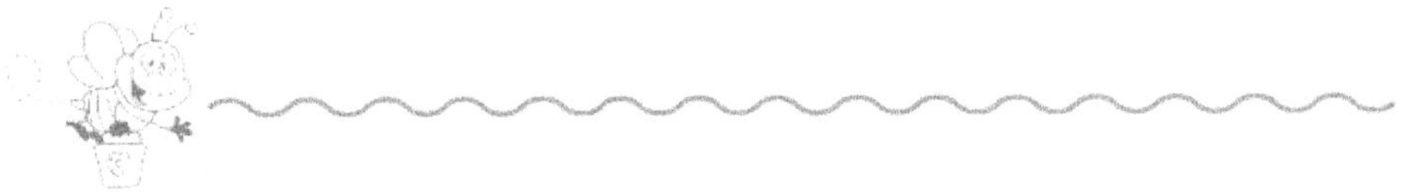

The number "five" is trying to give you a high five.

Ang bilang na "limang" ay sinusubukan na bigyan ka ng isang mataas na lima.

Name

I Can...

- [ ] read the 1st sentence.
- [ ] read the 2nd sentence.
- [ ] make a sentence from a picture.
- [ ] color a picture.
- [ ] Draw a picture.

My cat has four legs.

Ang aking pusa ay may apat na binti.

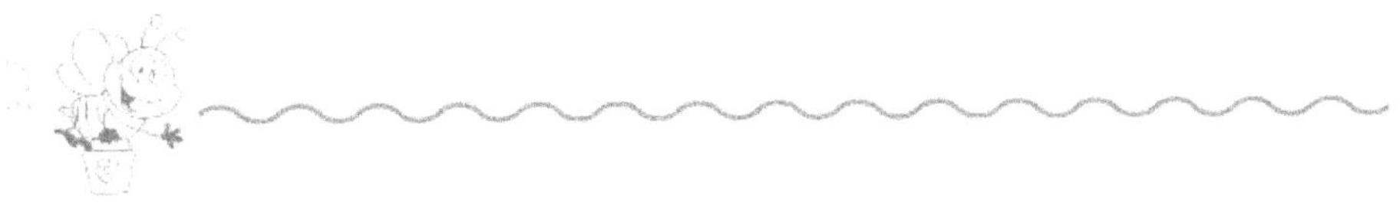

The number "four" is counting to four.

Ang bilang na "apat" ay nagbibilang sa apat.

A butterfly has six legs.

Ang isang butterfly ay may anim na binti.

The number "six" is saying 1+5=6.

Ang bilang ng "anim" ay nagsasabi ng 1 + 5 = 6.

Name

I Can...

- [ ] read the 1st sentence.
- [ ] read the 2nd sentence.
- [ ] make a sentence from a picture.
- [ ] color a picture.
- [ ] Draw a picture.

A spider has eight legs.

Ang isang spider ay may walong binti.

The happy and excited eight is holding up eight fingers

Ang masaya at nasasabik na walo ay may hawak na walong daliri

Name

I Can...

- [ ] read the 1st sentence.
- [ ] read the 2nd sentence.
- [ ] make a sentence from a picture.
- [ ] color a picture.
- [ ] Draw a picture.

The rooster is going to wake people up.

Gisingin ng manok ang mga tao.

The rooster is on the fence.

Ang tandang ay nasa bakod.

Name

I Can...

- [ ] read the 1st sentence.
- [ ] read the 2nd sentence.
- [ ] make a sentence from a picture.
- [ ] color a picture.
- [ ] Draw a picture.

My sister has nine stuffed animals.

Ang aking kapatid na babae ay may siyam na pinalamanan na hayop.

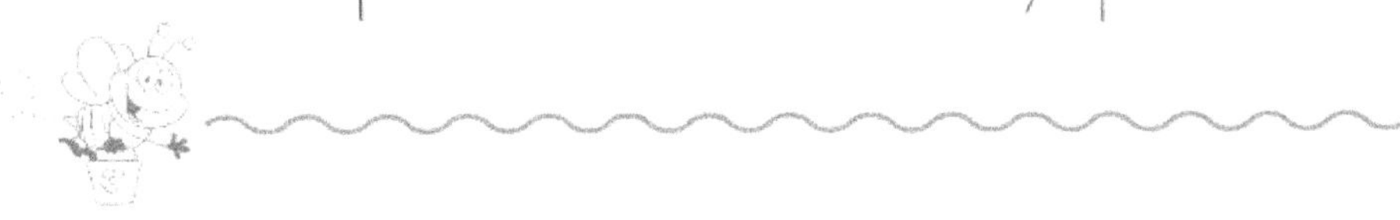

The smiling number nine is saying its name out loud.

Ang nakangiting numero siyam ay nagsasabing malakas ang pangalan nito.

Name

I Can...

- [ ] read the 1st sentence.
- [ ] read the 2nd sentence.
- [ ] make a sentence from a picture.
- [ ] color a picture.
- [ ] Draw a picture.

The baby bee has yellow and black stripes.

Ang bata na pukyutan ay may dilaw at itim na guhitan.

The bee is wearing a pink pacifier to calm itself.

Ang bubuyog ay may suot na pink na pacifier upang kalmado ang sarili.

Name

I Can...

- [ ] read the 1st sentence.
- [ ] read the 2nd sentence.
- [ ] make a sentence from a picture.
- [ ] color a picture.
- [ ] Draw a picture.

The ladybug has many spots.

Ang ladybug ay maraming mga spot.

The red and black ladybug is just done eating some leaves.

Ang pula at itim na ladybug ay tapos na kumain ng ilang mga dahon.

Name

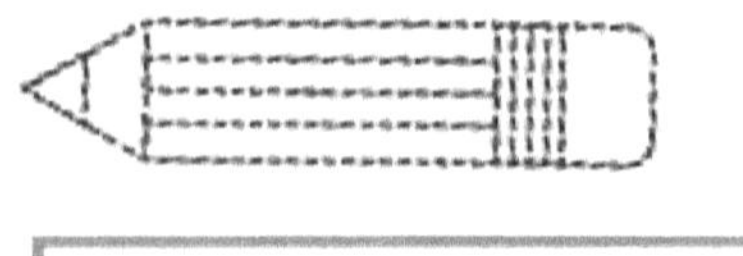

I Can...

- [ ] read the 1st sentence.
- [ ] read the 2nd sentence.
- [ ] make a sentence from a picture.
- [ ] color a picture.
- [ ] Draw a picture.

The sheep are skinny.

Ang mga tupa ay payat.

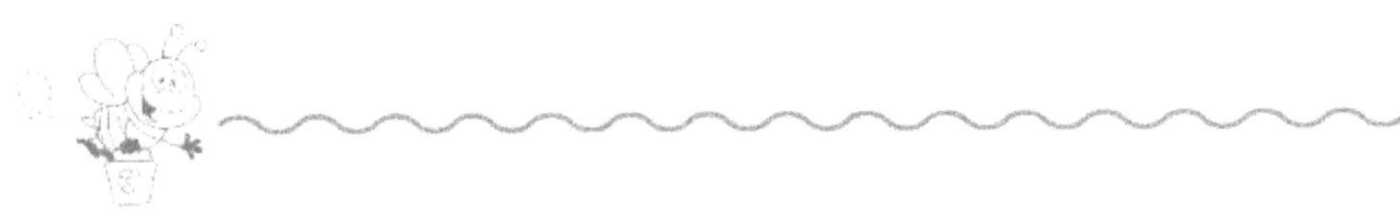

The white sheep have a lot of fluffy white wool to give away.

Ang mga puting tupa ay maraming malambot na puting balahibo upang ibigay.

Name

I Can...

- [ ] read the 1st sentence.
- [ ] read the 2nd sentence.
- [ ] make a sentence from a picture.
- [ ] color a picture.
- [ ] Draw a picture.

The rabbit is entering an egg painting contest.

Ang kuneho ay pumapasok sa isang paligsahan ng pagpipinta ng itlog.

The Easter Bunny is painting a chocolate egg.

Ang Easter Bunny ay nagpipinta ng isang itlog ng tsokolate.

Name

I Can...

- ☐ read the 1st sentence.
- ☐ read the 2nd sentence.
- ☐ make a sentence from a picture.
- ☐ color a picture.
- ☐ Draw a picture.

The owl is a language arts teacher.

Ang kuwago ay isang guro sa sining ng wika.

An owl is teaching the kids in school about work.

Ang isang kuwago ay nagtuturo sa mga bata sa paaralan tungkol sa trabaho.

Name

I Can...

- [ ] read the 1st sentence.
- [ ] read the 2nd sentence.
- [ ] make a sentence from a picture.
- [ ] color a picture.
- [ ] Draw a picture.

The man has an ancient hammer.

Ang tao ay may isang sinaunang martilyo.

The builder man has gone to work on a project.

Ang taong nagtayo ay napunta upang magtrabaho sa isang proyekto.

Name

I Can...

- [ ] read the 1st sentence.
- [ ] read the 2nd sentence.
- [ ] make a sentence from a picture.
- [ ] color a picture.
- [ ] Draw a picture.

The goat has a friend.

Ang kambing ay may kaibigan.

The old goat is proud of its golden bell.

Ipinagmamalaki ng matandang kambing sa gintong kampanilya nito.

Name

I Can...

- ☐ read the 1st sentence.
- ☐ read the 2nd sentence.
- ☐ make a sentence from a picture.
- ☐ color a picture.
- ☐ Draw a picture.

My mom's friend is a maid.

Kaibigan ng aking ina ay katulong.

The maid is going to clean the hotel room.

Pupunta ang dalaga sa paglilinis ng silid ng hotel.

Name ____________________ 

I Can...

- [ ] read the 1st sentence.
- [ ] read the 2nd sentence.
- [ ] make a sentence from a picture.
- [ ] color a picture.
- [ ] Draw a picture.

I went to the zoo.

Pumunta ako sa zoo.

The animals are having a big celebration.

Ang mga hayop ay nagkakaroon ng isang malaking pagdiriwang.

Name

I Can...

- [ ] read the 1st sentence.
- [ ] read the 2nd sentence.
- [ ] make a sentence from a picture.
- [ ] color a picture.
- [ ] Draw a picture.

The dinosaur has a pillow.

Ang unosaur ay may unan.

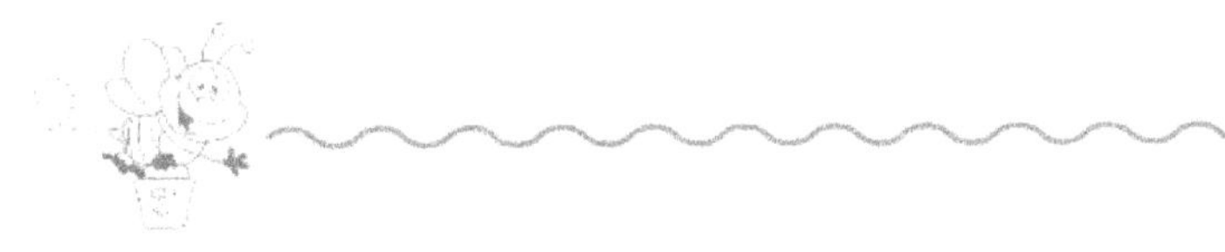

The dragon is using the rock to build its house.

Ang dragon ay gumagamit ng bato upang itayo ang bahay nito.

Name

I Can...

- [ ] read the 1st sentence.
- [ ] read the 2nd sentence.
- [ ] make a sentence from a picture.
- [ ] color a picture.
- [ ] Draw a picture.

The boy is excited to go to school.

Excited ang bata na pumasok sa paaralan.

The boy is late for school, so he is sprinting.

Ang batang lalaki ay huli na para sa paaralan, kaya siya ay sprinting.

Name

I Can...

- [ ] read the 1st sentence.
- [ ] read the 2nd sentence.
- [ ] make a sentence from a picture.
- [ ] color a picture.
- [ ] Draw a picture.

The kids on the school bus are going to school.

Ang mga bata sa bus ng paaralan ay pupunta sa paaralan.

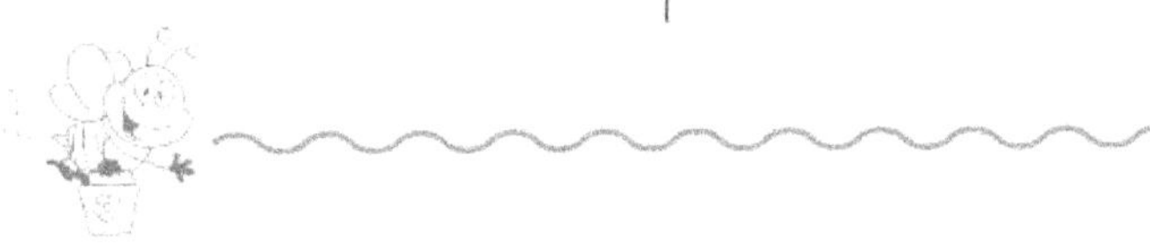

The children are going on a field trip on the yellow bus.

Ang mga bata ay pupunta sa isang field trip sa dilaw na bus.

Name

I Can...

- [ ] read the 1st sentence.
- [ ] read the 2nd sentence.
- [ ] make a sentence from a picture.
- [ ] color a picture.
- [ ] Draw a picture.

The cobra is very lovely.

Ang kobra ay napakaganda.

The rattlesnake is looking for its dinner.

Hinahanap ng rattlesnake ang hapunan nito.

Name

I Can...

- [ ] read the 1st sentence.
- [ ] read the 2nd sentence.
- [ ] make a sentence from a picture.
- [ ] color a picture.
- [ ] Draw a picture.

That is a fat dog!

Iyon ay isang taba na aso!

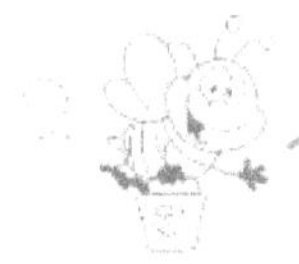

This dog is wagging its tail for more treats.

Ang aso na ito ay pinahuhulaan ang buntot nito para sa higit pang mga paggamot.

Name

I Can...

- ☐ read the 1st sentence.
- ☐ read the 2nd sentence.
- ☐ make a sentence from a picture.
- ☐ color a picture.
- ☐ Draw a picture.

The elephant lives in the zoo.

Ang elepante ay nakatira sa zoo.

The elephant has a long trunk to spray water.

Ang elepante ay may mahabang puno ng kahoy upang mag-spray ng tubig.

Name

I Can...

- [ ] read the 1st sentence.
- [ ] read the 2nd sentence.
- [ ] make a sentence from a picture.
- [ ] color a picture.
- [ ] Draw a picture.

The giraffe eats vegetables.

Kumakain ng gulay ang giraffe.

 ~~~~~~~~~~~~~~~~~~~~~~~~~~~~~~~~~~~

The giraffe has an extremely long neck.

Ang giraffe ay may sobrang haba ng leeg.

Name ________________

I Can...

- [ ] read the 1st sentence.
- [ ] read the 2nd sentence.
- [ ] make a sentence from a picture.
- [ ] color a picture.
- [ ] Draw a picture.

The chipmunk has a soft tummy.

Ang chipmunk ay may malambot na tummy.

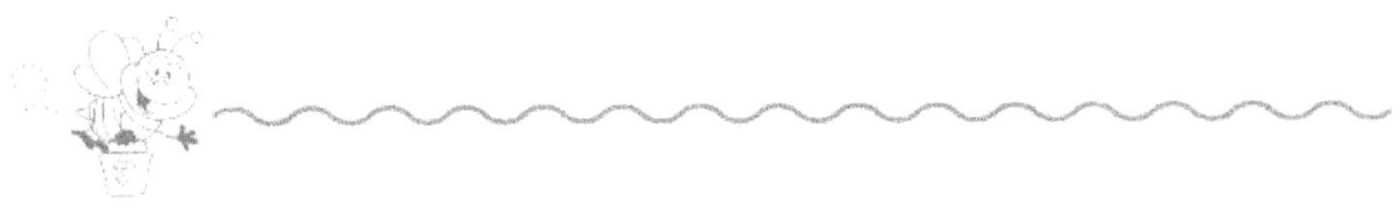

The Chipmunk is about to eat a brown acorn.

Ang Chipmunk ay malapit nang kumain ng isang brown acorn.

Name

I Can...

- [ ] read the 1st sentence.
- [ ] read the 2nd sentence.
- [ ] make a sentence from a picture.
- [ ] color a picture.
- [ ] Draw a picture.

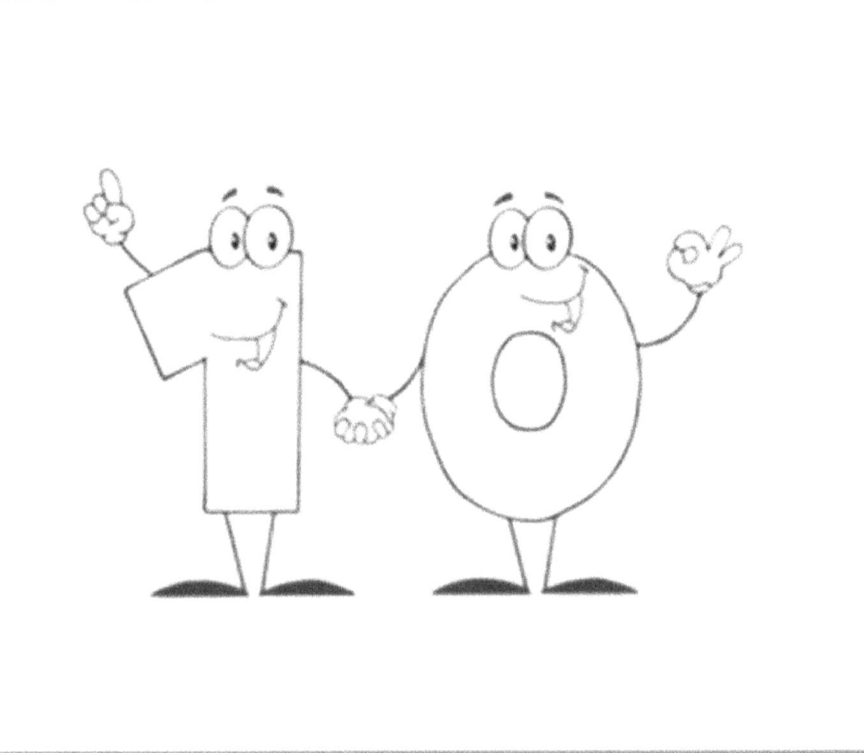

I have ten toes in total.

Mayroon akong sampung daliri sa kabuuan.

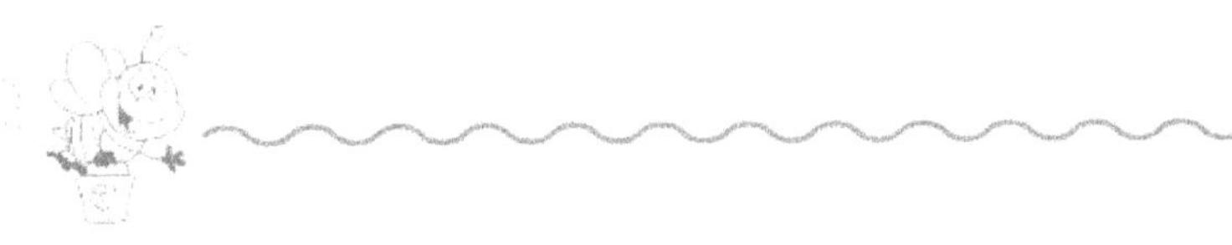

The one and the zero are holding hands.

Ang isa at ang zero ay may mga kamay.

Name

I Can...

- [ ] read the 1st sentence.
- [ ] read the 2nd sentence.
- [ ] make a sentence from a picture.
- [ ] color a picture.
- [ ] Draw a picture.

The alligator is jumping.

Tumalon ang alligator.

The crocodile is excited.

Natutuwa ang buwaya.

Name

I Can...

- [ ] read the 1st sentence.
- [ ] read the 2nd sentence.
- [ ] make a sentence from a picture.
- [ ] color a picture.
- [ ] Draw a picture.

I found an ant.

May nakita akong ant.

The ant is telling a story.

Ang langgam ay nagsasabi ng isang kuwento.

Name ______________

I Can...

- [ ] read the 1st sentence.
- [ ] read the 2nd sentence.
- [ ] make a sentence from a picture.
- [ ] color a picture.
- [ ] Draw a picture.

The bat sleeps upside down.

Ang bat ay natutulog baligtad.

The bat is ready to fly.

Ang bat ay handa nang lumipad.

Name

I Can...

- [ ] read the 1st sentence.
- [ ] read the 2nd sentence.
- [ ] make a sentence from a picture.
- [ ] color a picture.
- [ ] Draw a picture.

The cat is very tired.

Ang pusa ay sobrang pagod.

The cat is taking a nap.

Nakakatulog ang pusa.

Name

I Can...

- [ ] read the 1st sentence.
- [ ] read the 2nd sentence.
- [ ] make a sentence from a picture.
- [ ] color a picture.
- [ ] Draw a picture.

The dog likes to play.

Mahilig maglaro ang aso.

The dog is playing with a bone.

Ang aso ay naglalaro na may isang buto.

Name

I Can...

- [ ] read the 1st sentence.
- [ ] read the 2nd sentence.
- [ ] make a sentence from a picture.
- [ ] color a picture.
- [ ] Draw a picture.

The elephant has eyelashes.

Ang mga elepante ay may eyelashes.

The elephant is shy.

Nahihiya ang elepante.

Name

I Can...

- [ ] read the 1st sentence.
- [ ] read the 2nd sentence.
- [ ] make a sentence from a picture.
- [ ] color a picture.
- [ ] Draw a picture.

The frog is hopping.

Ang palaka ay humihinto.

The frog is trying to catch the fly.

Ang palaka ay sinusubukan upang mahuli ang fly.

Name

I Can...

- [ ] read the 1st sentence.
- [ ] read the 2nd sentence.
- [ ] make a sentence from a picture.
- [ ] color a picture.
- [ ] Draw a picture.

The goat is sleepily walking around.

Ang kambing ay natutulog na naglalakad sa paligid.

The goat is eating grass.

Ang kambing ay kumakain ng damo.

Name

I Can...

- [ ] read the 1st sentence.
- [ ] read the 2nd sentence.
- [ ] make a sentence from a picture.
- [ ] color a picture.
- [ ] Draw a picture.

The hippo has a big head.

Ang hippo ay may malaking ulo.

The hippo has a big head.

Ang hippo ay may malaking ulo.

I Can...

- [ ] read the 1st sentence.
- [ ] read the 2nd sentence.
- [ ] make a sentence from a picture.
- [ ] color a picture.
- [ ] Draw a picture.

The iguana has a long tail.

Ang iguana ay may mahabang buntot.

 ~~~~~~~~~~~~~~~~~~~~~~~~~~~~~~~~~~~~~~

The iguana is hiding behind the letter I.

Nagtago ang iguana sa likuran ng liham I.

Name ____________________

I Can...

- [ ] read the 1st sentence.
- [ ] read the 2nd sentence.
- [ ] make a sentence from a picture.
- [ ] color a picture.
- [ ] Draw a picture.

Mom bought a new bottle of jam.

Bumili si Nanay ng bagong bote ng jam.

 ~~~~~~~~~~~~~~~~~~~~~~~~~~~~~~~~~~~~~~

There is jam on the bread.

May jam sa tinapay.

Name

I Can...

- [ ] read the 1st sentence.
- [ ] read the 2nd sentence.
- [ ] make a sentence from a picture.
- [ ] color a picture.
- [ ] Draw a picture.

The kite has a beautiful tail.

Ang saranggola ay may magandang buntot.

The kite is on the ground.

Ang saranggola ay nasa lupa.

Name

I Can...

- [ ] read the 1st sentence.
- [ ] read the 2nd sentence.
- [ ] make a sentence from a picture.
- [ ] color a picture.
- [ ] Draw a picture.

The lion is timid.

Ang leon ay mahiyain.

The lion is big.

Malaki ang leon.

Name

I Can...

- ☐ read the 1st sentence.
- ☐ read the 2nd sentence.
- ☐ make a sentence from a picture.
- ☐ color a picture.
- ☐ Draw a picture.

I like mice.

Gusto ko ng mga daga.

A rat is on top of the letter M

Ang isang daga ay nasa itaas ng titik M

Name

I Can...

- [ ] read the 1st sentence.
- [ ] read the 2nd sentence.
- [ ] make a sentence from a picture.
- [ ] color a picture.
- [ ] Draw a picture.

The nose is breathing.

Huminga ang ilong.

The letter N stands for a nose.

Ang letrang N ay nangangahulugang ilong.

Name

I Can...

- [ ] read the 1st sentence.
- [ ] read the 2nd sentence.
- [ ] make a sentence from a picture.
- [ ] color a picture.
- [ ] Draw a picture.

The octopus lives underwater.

Ang pugita ay nabubuhay sa ilalim ng dagat.

The octopus has eight tentacles.

Ang kctopus ay may walong tent tent.

Name

I Can...

- [ ] read the 1st sentence.
- [ ] read the 2nd sentence.
- [ ] make a sentence from a picture.
- [ ] color a picture.
- [ ] Draw a picture.

The penguin eats fish.

Ang penguin ay kumakain ng isda.

The penguin lives in the arctic.

Ang penguin ay nakatira sa arctic.

Name

I Can...

- [ ] read the 1st sentence.
- [ ] read the 2nd sentence.
- [ ] make a sentence from a picture.
- [ ] color a picture.
- [ ] Draw a picture.

The queen has a wand.

Ang reyna ay may isang wand.

The queen is beautiful.

Maganda ang reyna.

Name

I Can...

- [ ] read the 1st sentence.
- [ ] read the 2nd sentence.
- [ ] make a sentence from a picture.
- [ ] color a picture.
- [ ] Draw a picture.

The rabbit has long ears.

Ang kuneho ay may mahabang mga tainga.

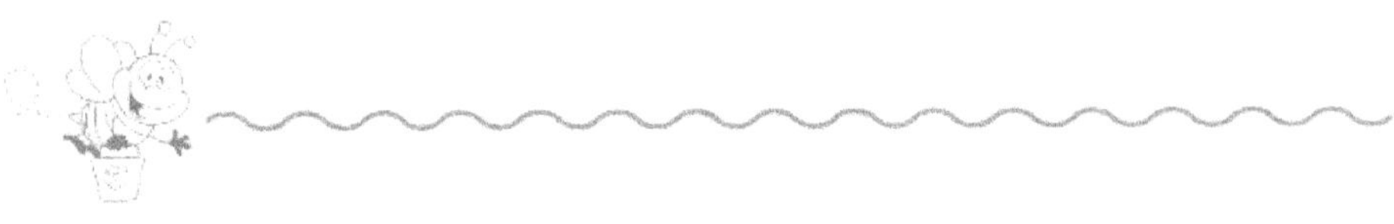

The rabbit is thinking about something.

Ang kuneho ay nag-iisip tungkol sa isang bagay.

Name

I Can...

- [ ] read the 1st sentence.
- [ ] read the 2nd sentence.
- [ ] make a sentence from a picture.
- [ ] color a picture.
- [ ] Draw a picture.

The snake has polka dots.

Ang ahas ay may polka tuldok.

The snake is licking its lip because it is hungry.

Ang ahas ay dumila ang labi nito dahil gutom na.

Name

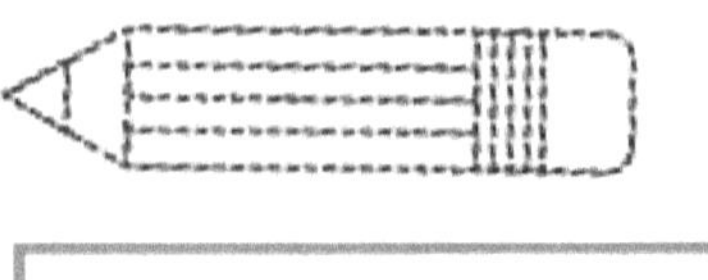

I Can...

- [ ] read the 1st sentence.
- [ ] read the 2nd sentence.
- [ ] make a sentence from a picture.
- [ ] color a picture.
- [ ] Draw a picture.

The tortoise has a pointy shell.

Ang pagong ay may isang pointy shell.

The turtle has a robust shell but is very slow.

Ang pagong ay may matibay na shell ngunit napakabagal.

Name 

I Can...

- ☐ read the 1st sentence.
- ☐ read the 2nd sentence.
- ☐ make a sentence from a picture.
- ☐ color a picture.
- ☐ Draw a picture. 

It's raining.

Umuulan.

 ～～～～～～～～～～～～～

We use the umbrella when it's raining.

Ginagamit namin ang payong kapag umuulan.

Name ___________

I Can...

- [ ] read the 1st sentence.
- [ ] read the 2nd sentence.
- [ ] make a sentence from a picture.
- [ ] color a picture.
- [ ] Draw a picture.

The violin is a musical instrument.

Ang biyolin ay isang instrumento sa musika.

A violin can play beautiful music if played correctly.

Ang isang biyolin ay maaaring maglaro ng magagandang musika kung tama ang nilalaro.

Name

I Can...

- [ ] read the 1st sentence.
- [ ] read the 2nd sentence.
- [ ] make a sentence from a picture.
- [ ] color a picture.
- [ ] Draw a picture.

The walrus has a friend.

Ang walrus ay may kaibigan.

____

The walrus has unusually sharp teeth.

Ang walrus ay may hindi pangkaraniwang matalas na ngipin.

Name

I Can...

- [ ] read the 1st sentence.
- [ ] read the 2nd sentence.
- [ ] make a sentence from a picture.
- [ ] color a picture.
- [ ] Draw a picture.

The xylophone is a colorful instrument.

Ang xylophone ay isang makulay na instrumento.

The xylophone is an instrument like the piano.

Ang xylophone ay isang instrumento tulad ng piano.

I Can...

- [ ] read the 1st sentence.
- [ ] read the 2nd sentence.
- [ ] make a sentence from a picture.
- [ ] color a picture.
- [ ] Draw a picture.

The boy has a little hat.

Ang batang lalaki ay may isang maliit na sumbrero.

The boy is having fun playing with a yoyo.

Ang batang lalaki ay nakakatuwang naglalaro sa isang yoyo.

Name

I Can...

- [ ] read the 1st sentence.
- [ ] read the 2nd sentence.
- [ ] make a sentence from a picture.
- [ ] color a picture.
- [ ] Draw a picture.

The zebra has a tail.

Ang zebra ay may isang buntot.

____

The zebra has black and white stripes.

Ang zebra ay may itim at puting guhitan.

Name ___________

I Can...

- ☐ read the 1st sentence.
- ☐ read the 2nd sentence.
- ☐ make a sentence from a picture.
- ☐ color a picture.
- ☐ Draw a picture.

I have a candle on my cake.

Mayroon akong kandila sa aking cake.

I had a small birthday cake for my party.

Nagkaroon ako ng isang maliit na cake ng kaarawan para sa aking pagdiriwang.

Name ___________

I Can...

- [ ] read the 1st sentence.
- [ ] read the 2nd sentence.
- [ ] make a sentence from a picture.
- [ ] color a picture.
- [ ] Draw a picture.

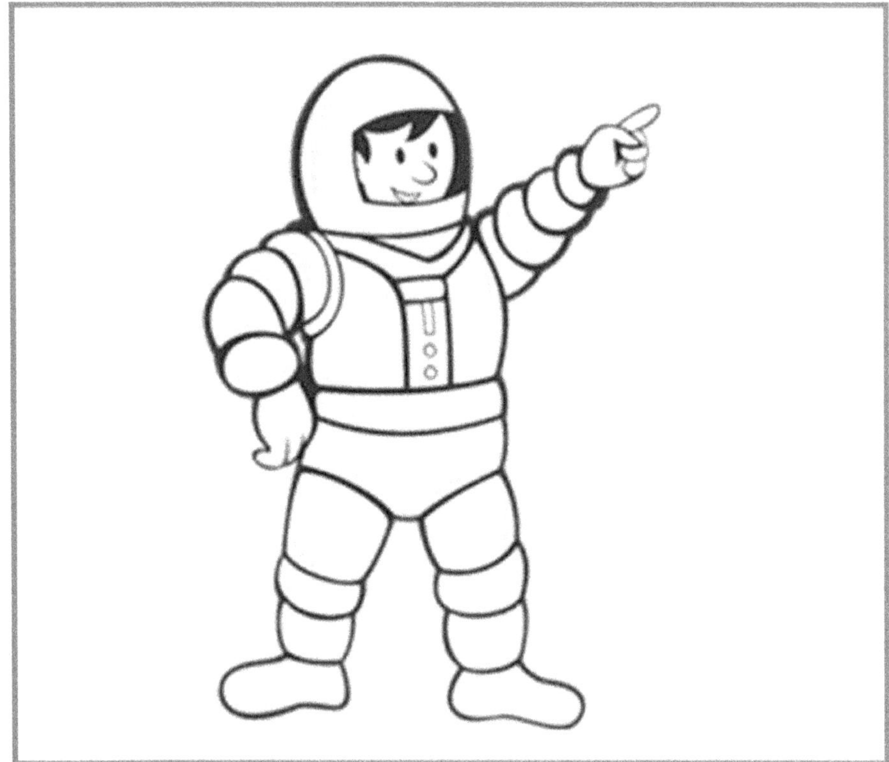

The astronaut is going on a mission.

Ang astronaut ay pupunta sa isang misyon.

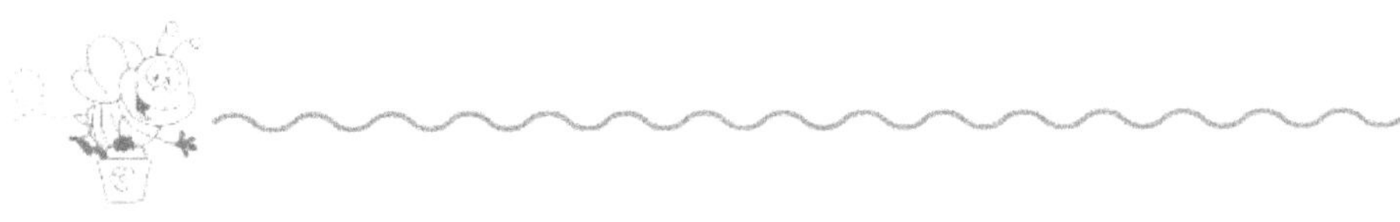

An astronaut has to explore our universe so that we would have more knowledge.

Ang isang astronaut ay dapat galugarin ang ating uniberso upang magkaroon tayo ng mas maraming kaalaman.

Name

I Can...

- [ ] read the 1st sentence.
- [ ] read the 2nd sentence.
- [ ] make a sentence from a picture.
- [ ] color a picture.
- [ ] Draw a picture.

The samurai is going for a morning jog.

Pupunta ang samurai para sa isang umaga na jog.

The samurai is training to become good at fighting.

Ang samurai ay pagsasanay upang maging mahusay sa pakikipaglaban.

Name

I Can...

- [ ] read the 1st sentence.
- [ ] read the 2nd sentence.
- [ ] make a sentence from a picture.
- [ ] color a picture.
- [ ] Draw a picture.

My friend is having a gigantic cake.

Ang aking kaibigan ay nagkakaroon ng isang napakalaking cake.

I had a humongous birthday cake for my celebration.

Mayroon akong isang nakakahiyang cake ng kaarawan para sa pagdiriwang ko.

Name

I Can...

- [ ] read the 1st sentence.
- [ ] read the 2nd sentence.
- [ ] make a sentence from a picture.
- [ ] color a picture.
- [ ] Draw a picture.

The frog is chasing the fly.

Hinahabol ng palaka ang fly.

The green frog is trying to catch the fly.

Ang berdeng palaka ay sinusubukan upang mahuli ang fly.

Name

I Can...

- [ ] read the 1st sentence.
- [ ] read the 2nd sentence.
- [ ] make a sentence from a picture.
- [ ] color a picture.
- [ ] Draw a picture.

The ladybug has six legs.

Ang ladybug ay may anim na binti.

The ladybug is on the leaf.

Ang ladybug ay nasa dahon.

Name

I Can...

- [ ] read the 1st sentence.
- [ ] read the 2nd sentence.
- [ ] make a sentence from a picture.
- [ ] color a picture.
- [ ] Draw a picture.

The dragon is sick.

May sakit ang dragon.

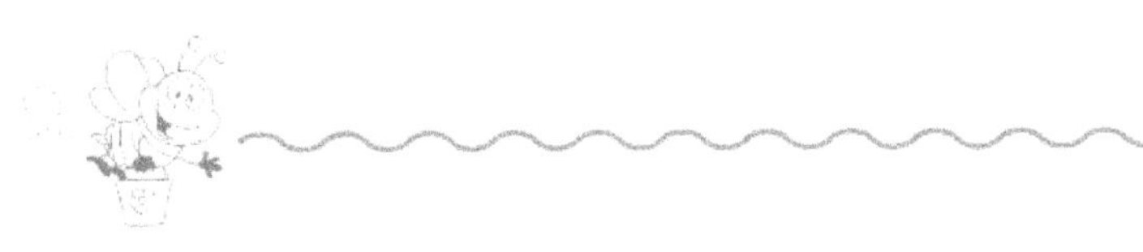

The dragon just ate something spicy, so he needed water.

Kumain lang ang dragon ng isang maanghang, kaya kailangan niya ng tubig.

Name

I Can...

- [ ] read the 1st sentence.
- [ ] read the 2nd sentence.
- [ ] make a sentence from a picture.
- [ ] color a picture.
- [ ] Draw a picture.

That is a baby cow.

Iyon ay isang sanggol na baka.

A little cow is walking around near the barn.

Ang isang maliit na baka ay naglalakad palapit sa kamalig.

Name

I Can...

- [ ] read the 1st sentence.
- [ ] read the 2nd sentence.
- [ ] make a sentence from a picture.
- [ ] color a picture.
- [ ] Draw a picture.

The frog has a big smile.

Ang palaka ay may malaking ngiti.

The frog is smiling because it is happy.

Nakangiti ang palaka dahil masaya ito.

Name

I Can...

- [ ] read the 1st sentence.
- [ ] read the 2nd sentence.
- [ ] make a sentence from a picture.
- [ ] color a picture.
- [ ] Draw a picture.

The frog has a big mouth.

May malaking bibig ang palaka.

The frog is waving to us.

Ang palaka ay kumakaway sa amin.